FLOWERS

by Eli Zagoria

I0483618

Other Booklets of Eli Zagoria's Art

PERTH AND SURROUND

ELI ZAGORIA'S ART

National Library of Australia Cataloguing-in-Publication entry
Title: FLOWERS by Eli Zagoria
ISBN: 9780987106346 (paperback)
Series: Eli Zagoria's Art
Subjects: Flowers Paintings Art Eli Zagoria
Other Authors/Contributors: nil
Dewey Number: 362.732089924
This edition first published February 2014

Copyright © David Solly Sandler 2014
E-mail: <sedsand@iinet.net.au>
ISBN 978-0-9871063-4-6

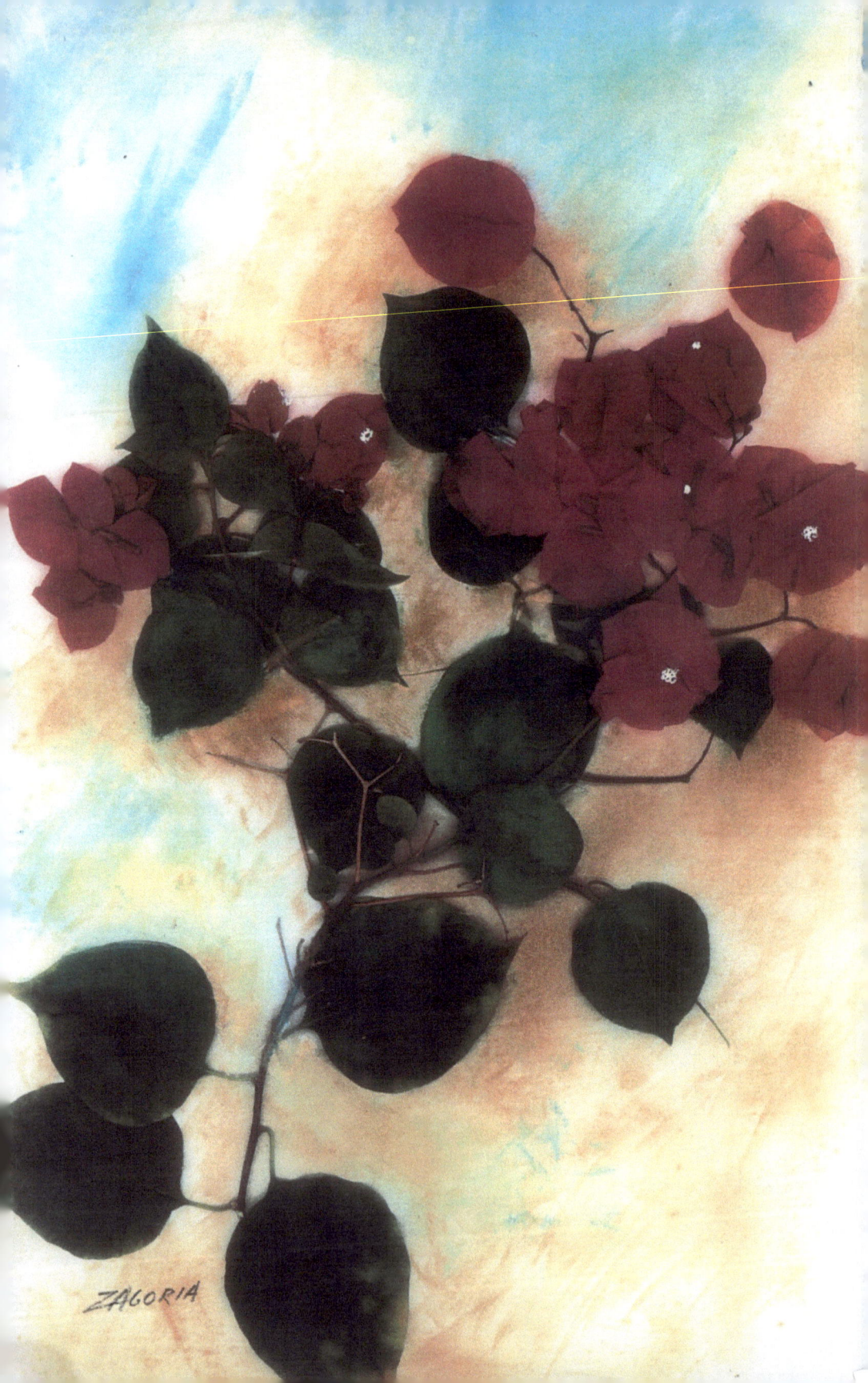

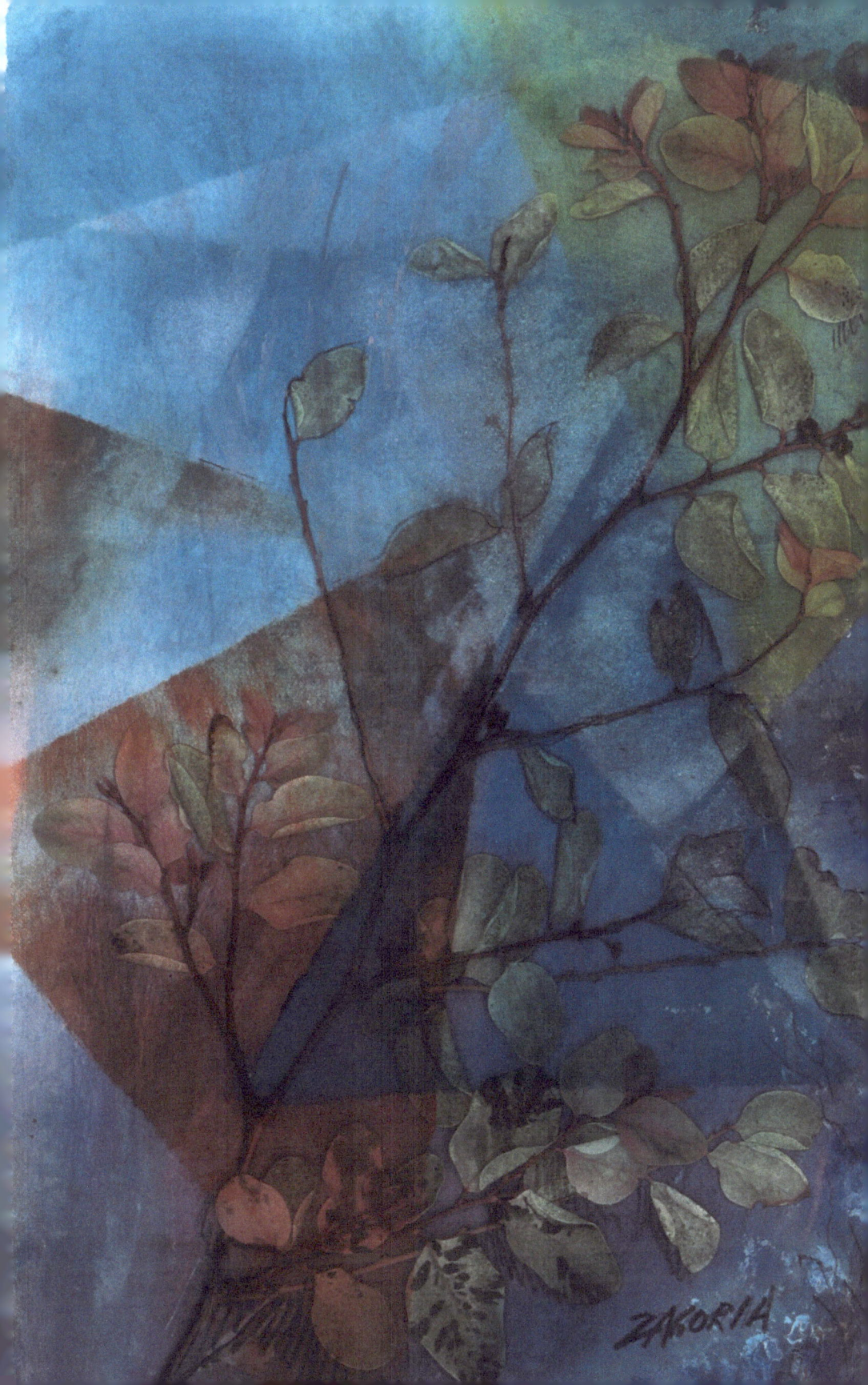

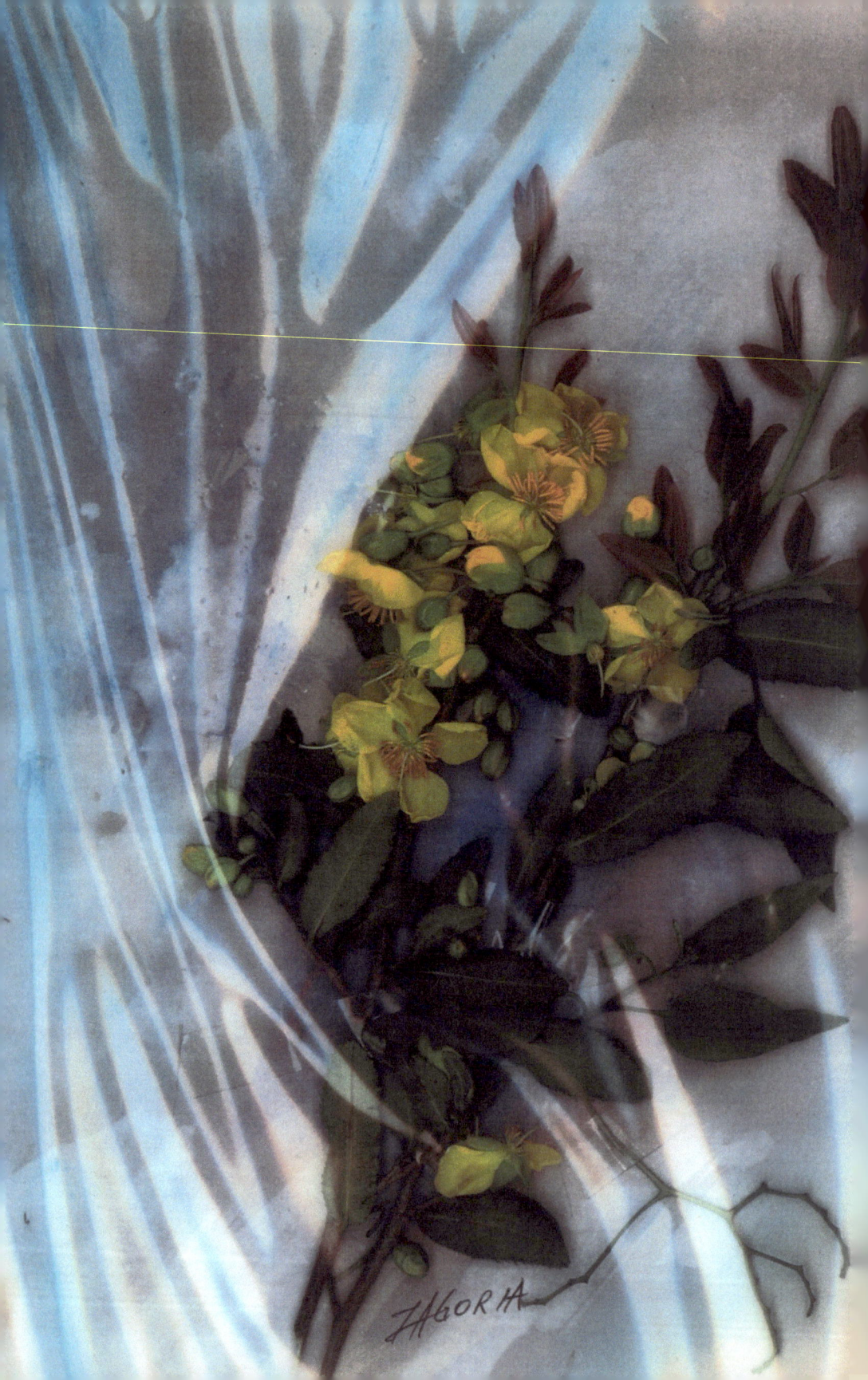

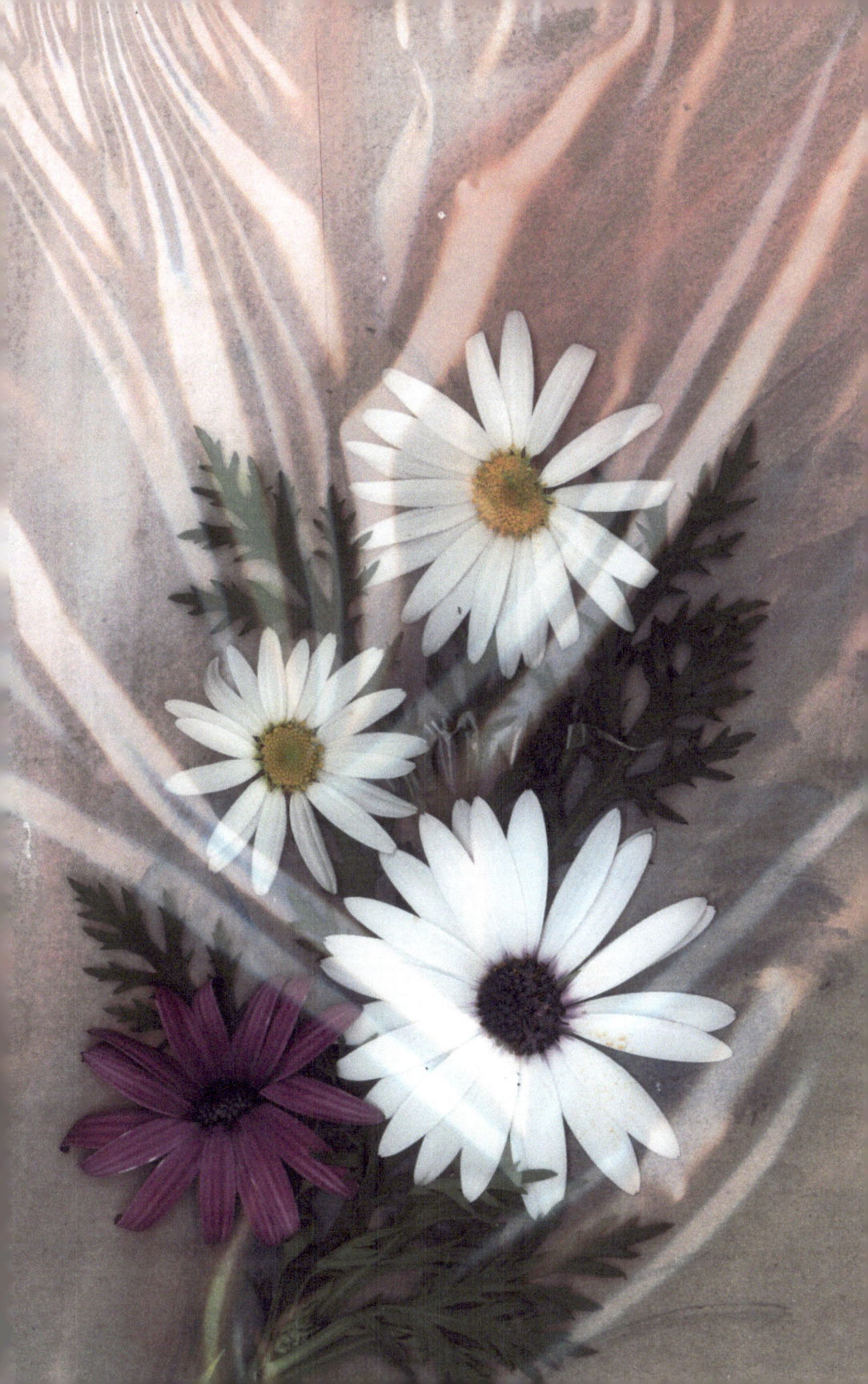

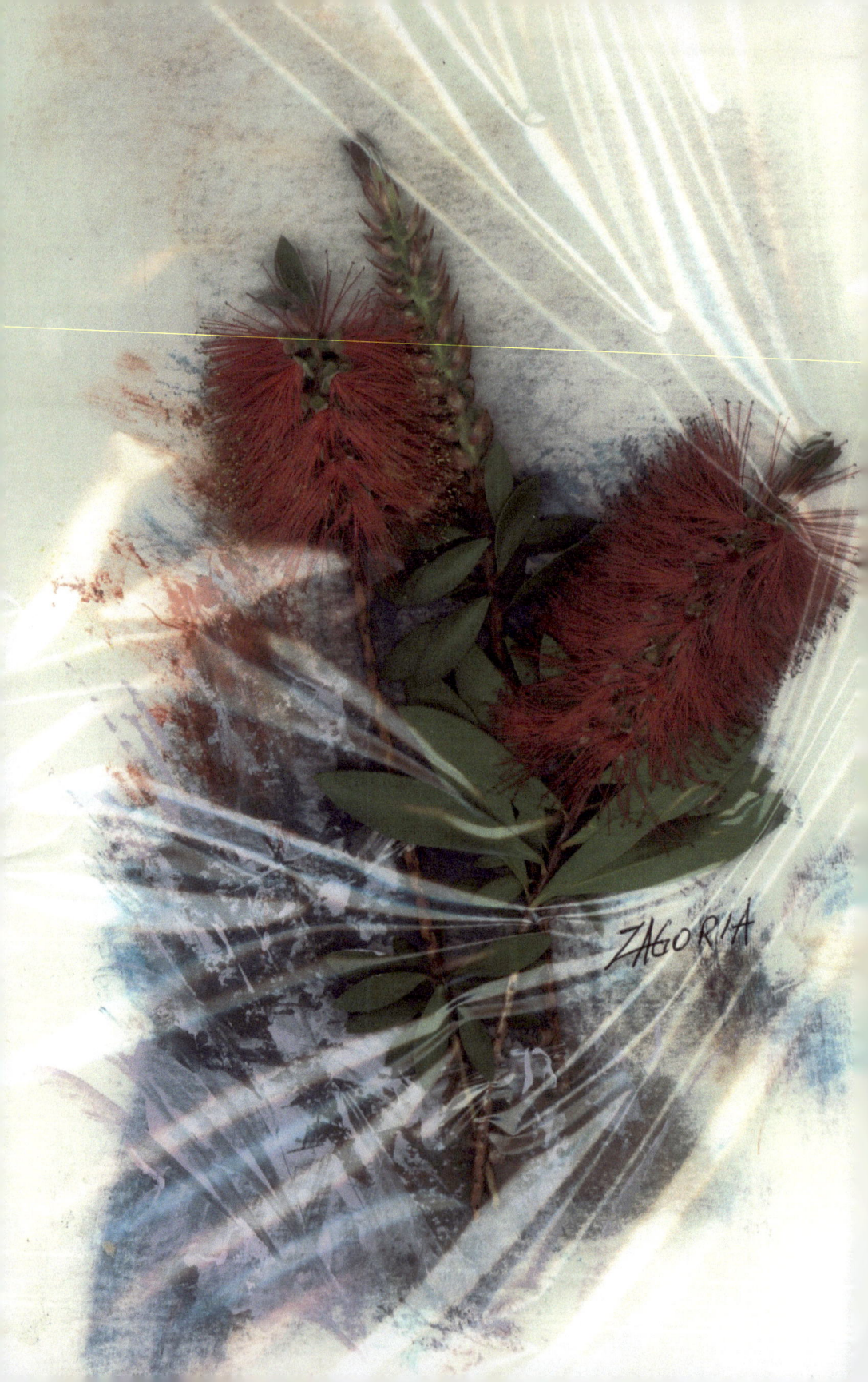

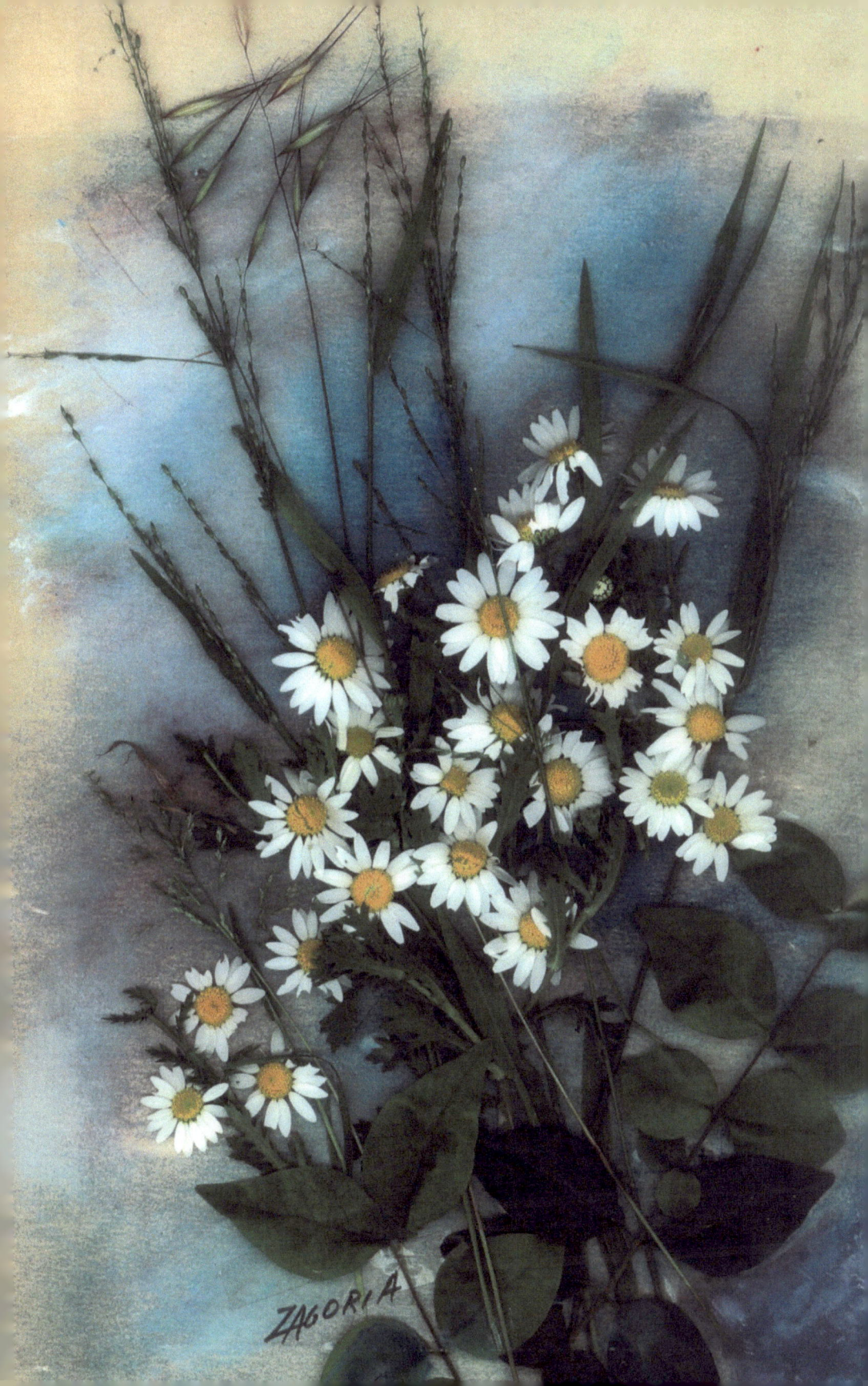

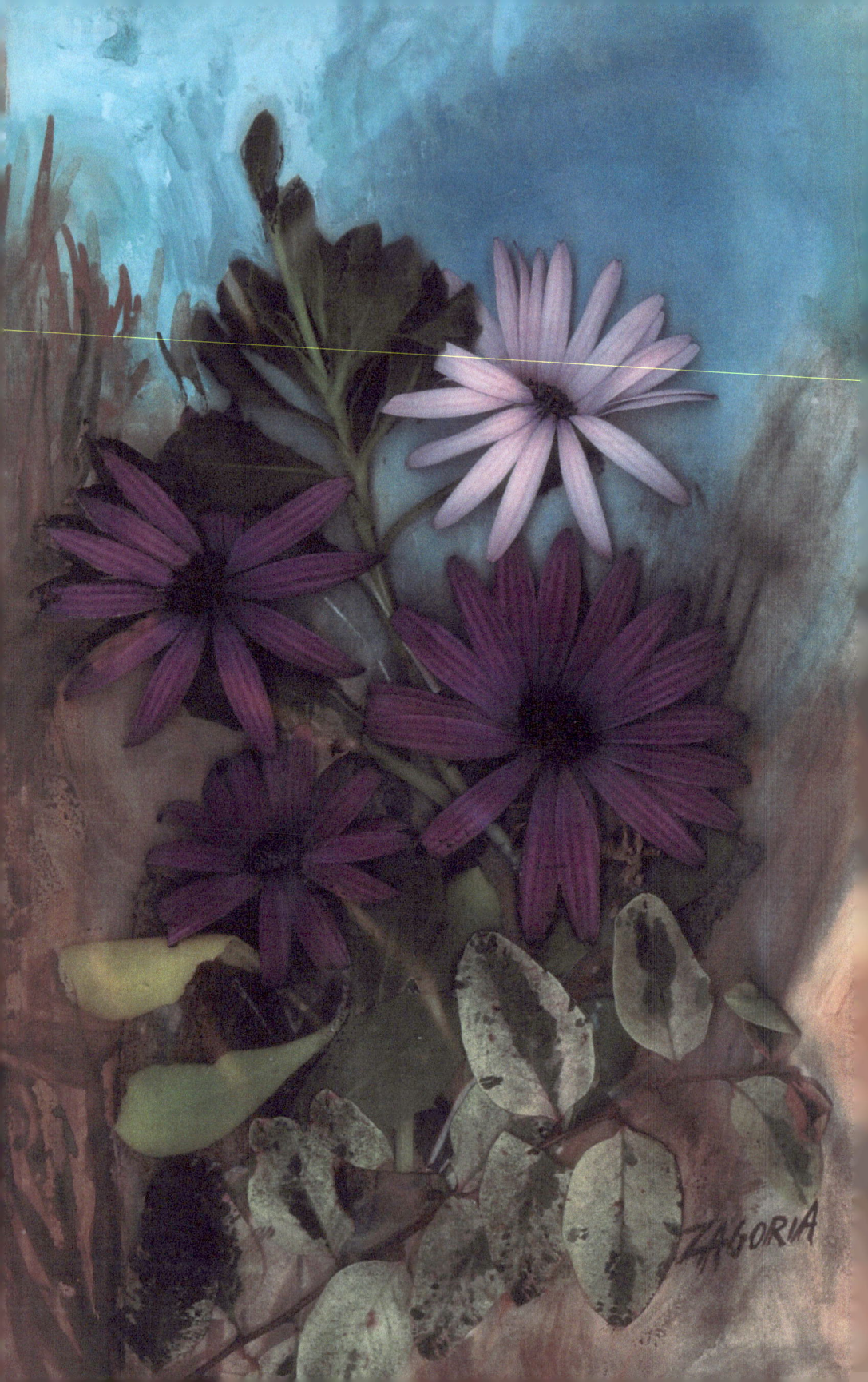

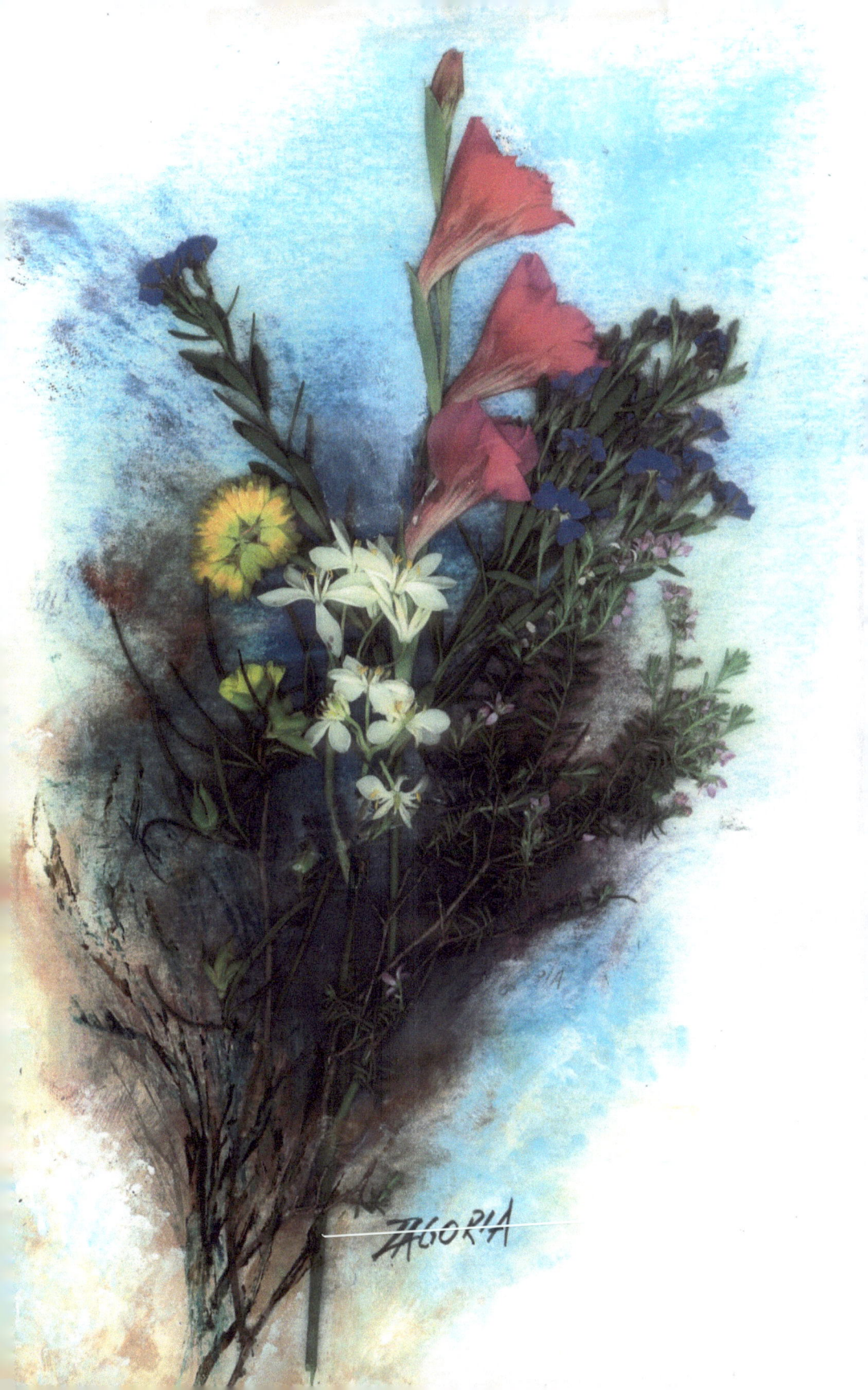

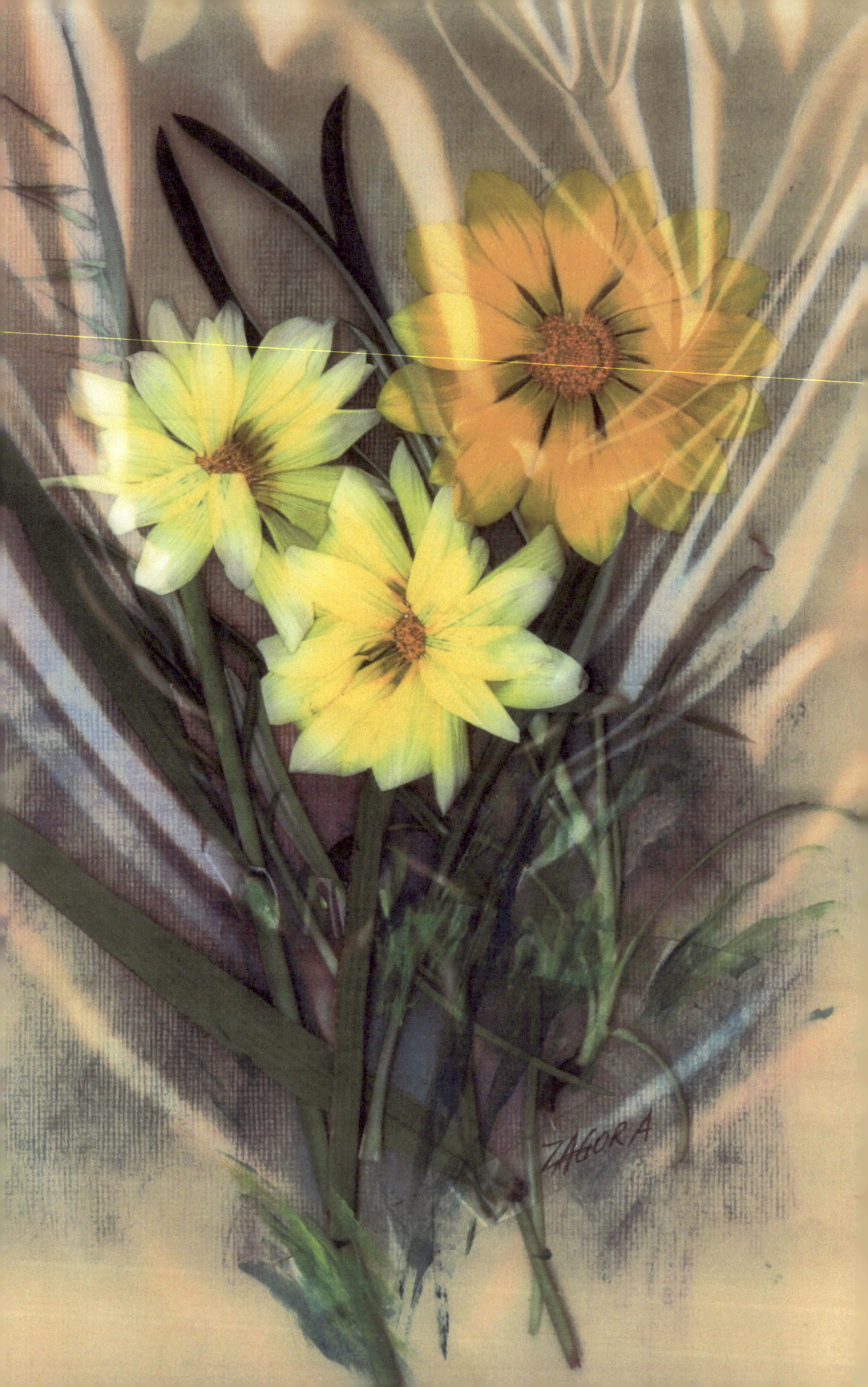

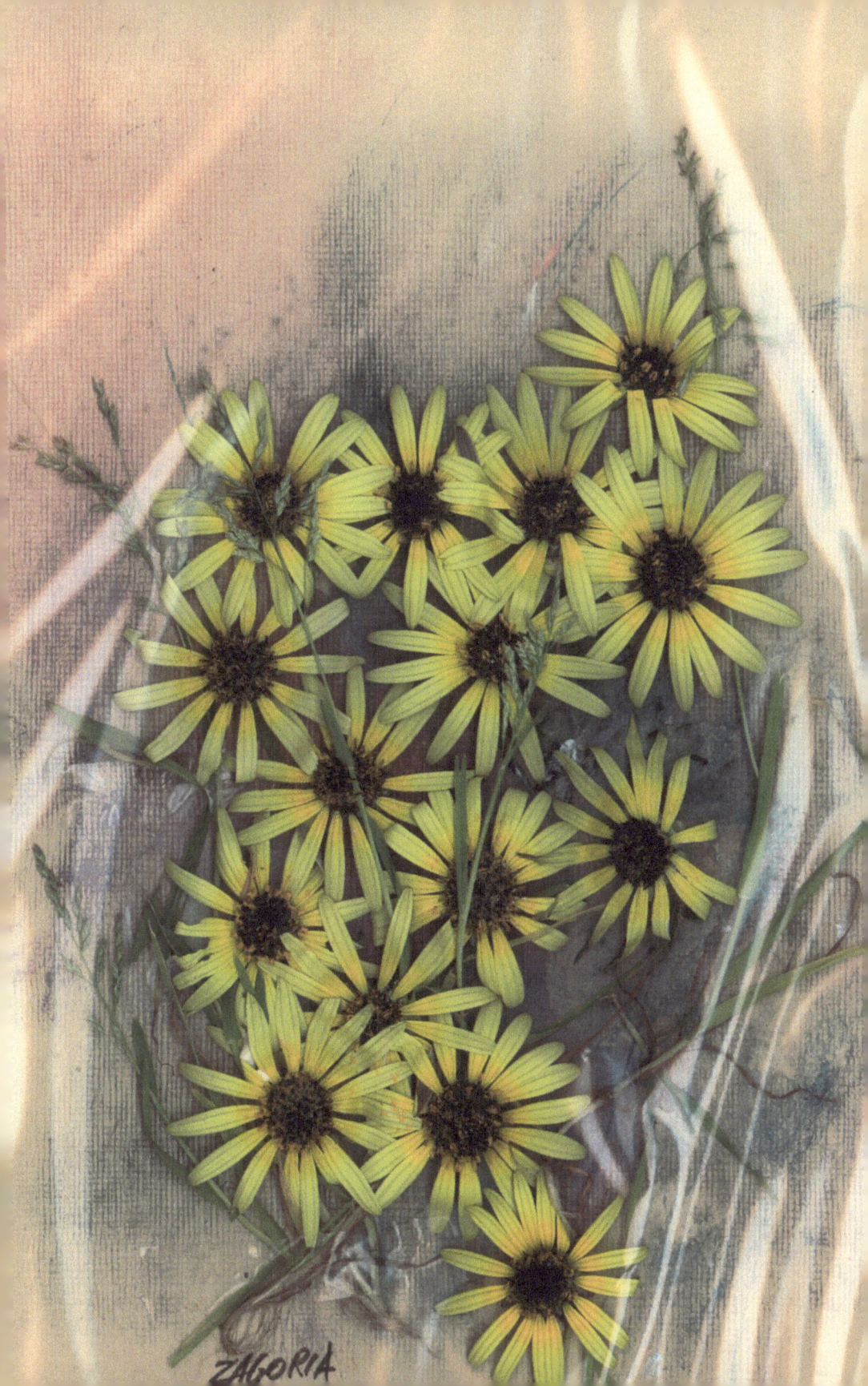

ZAGORIA

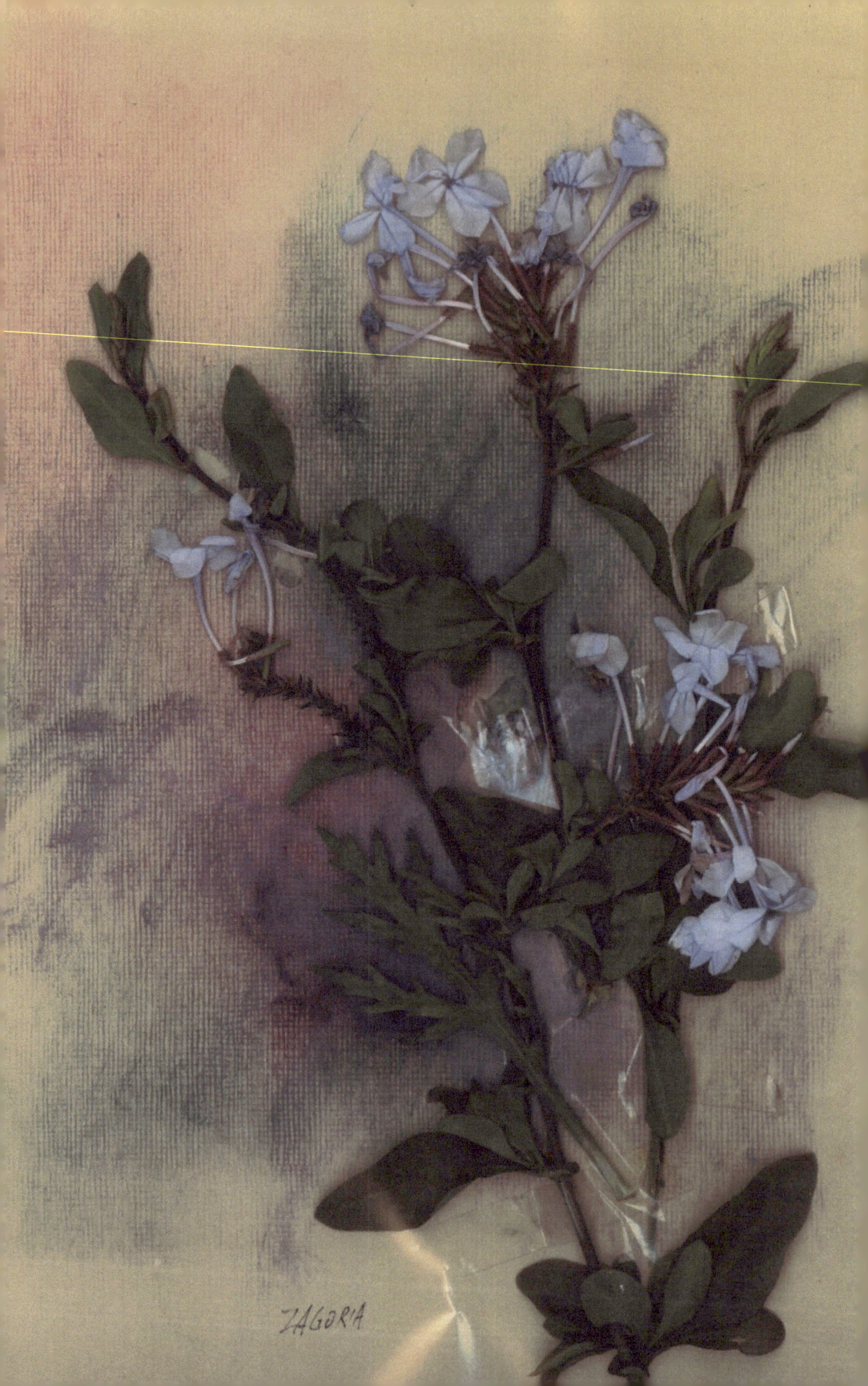

ZAGORA

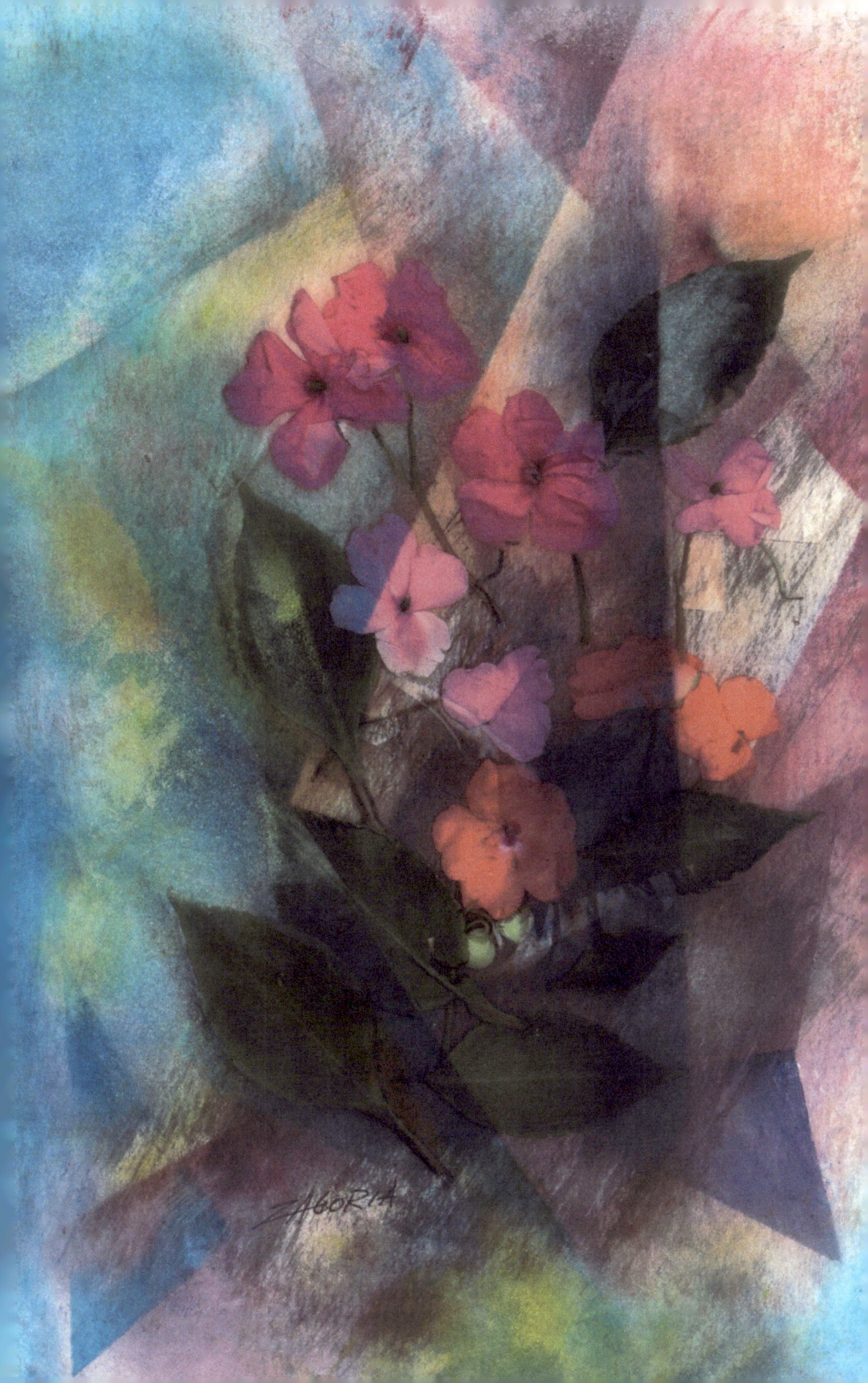

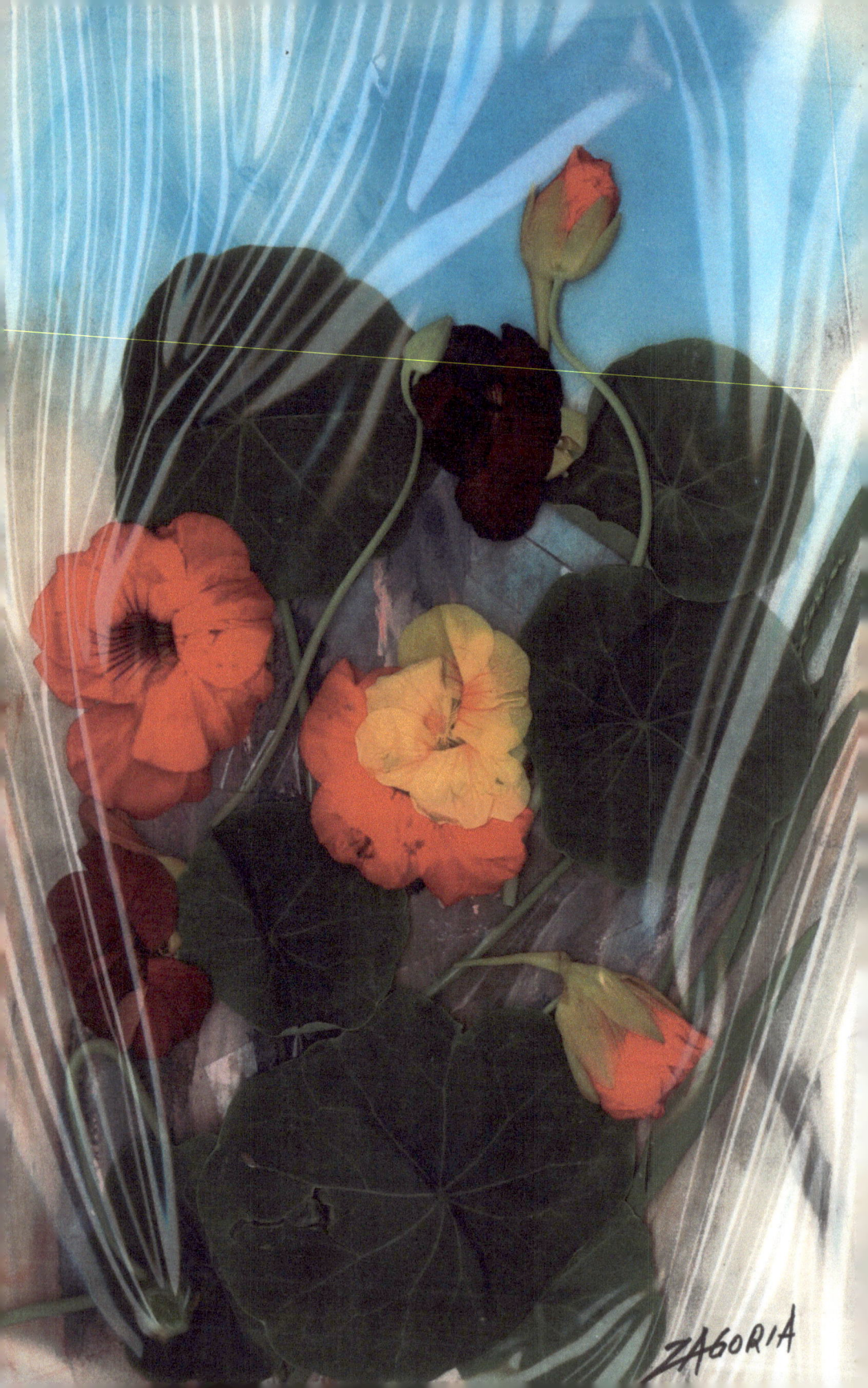

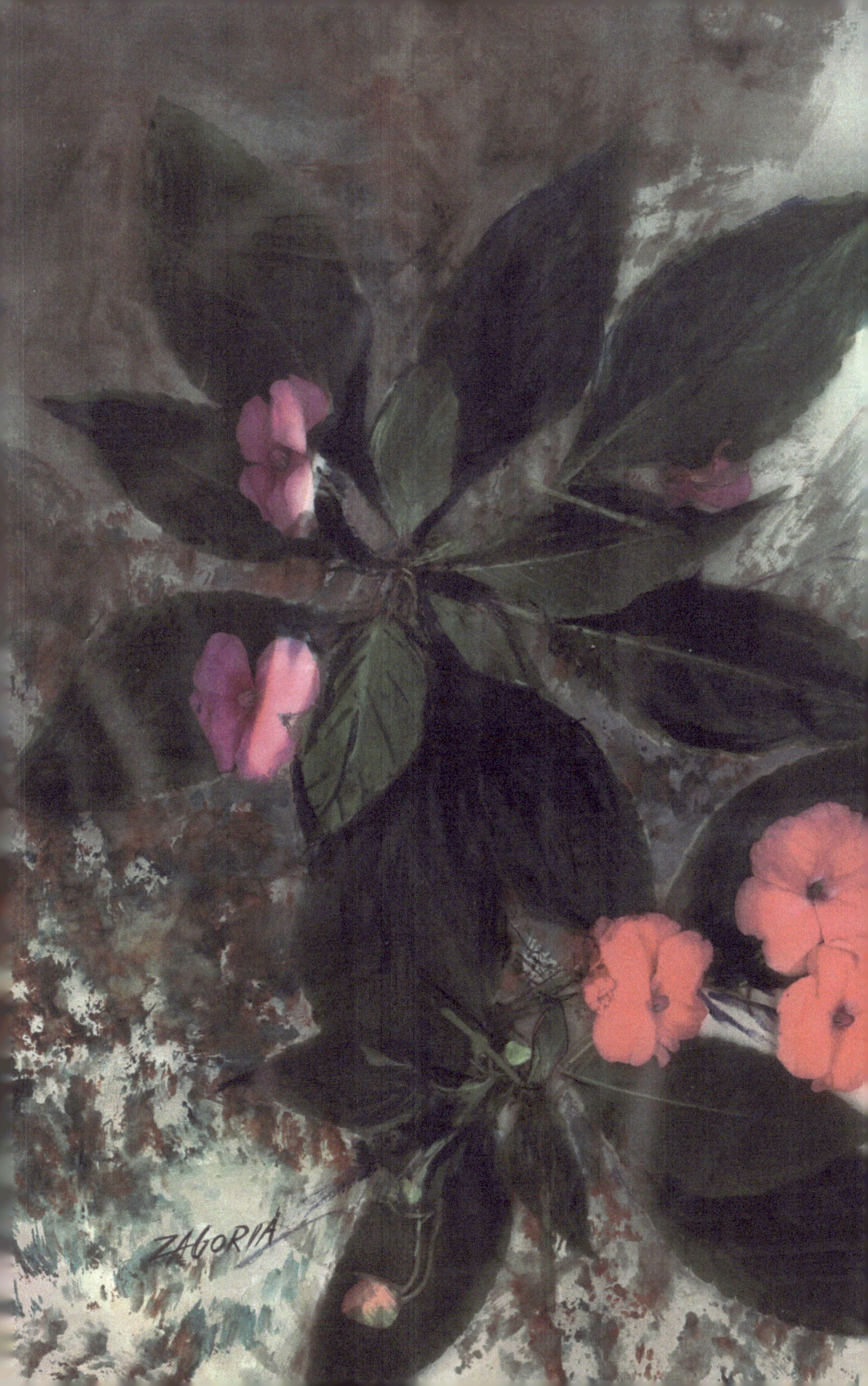

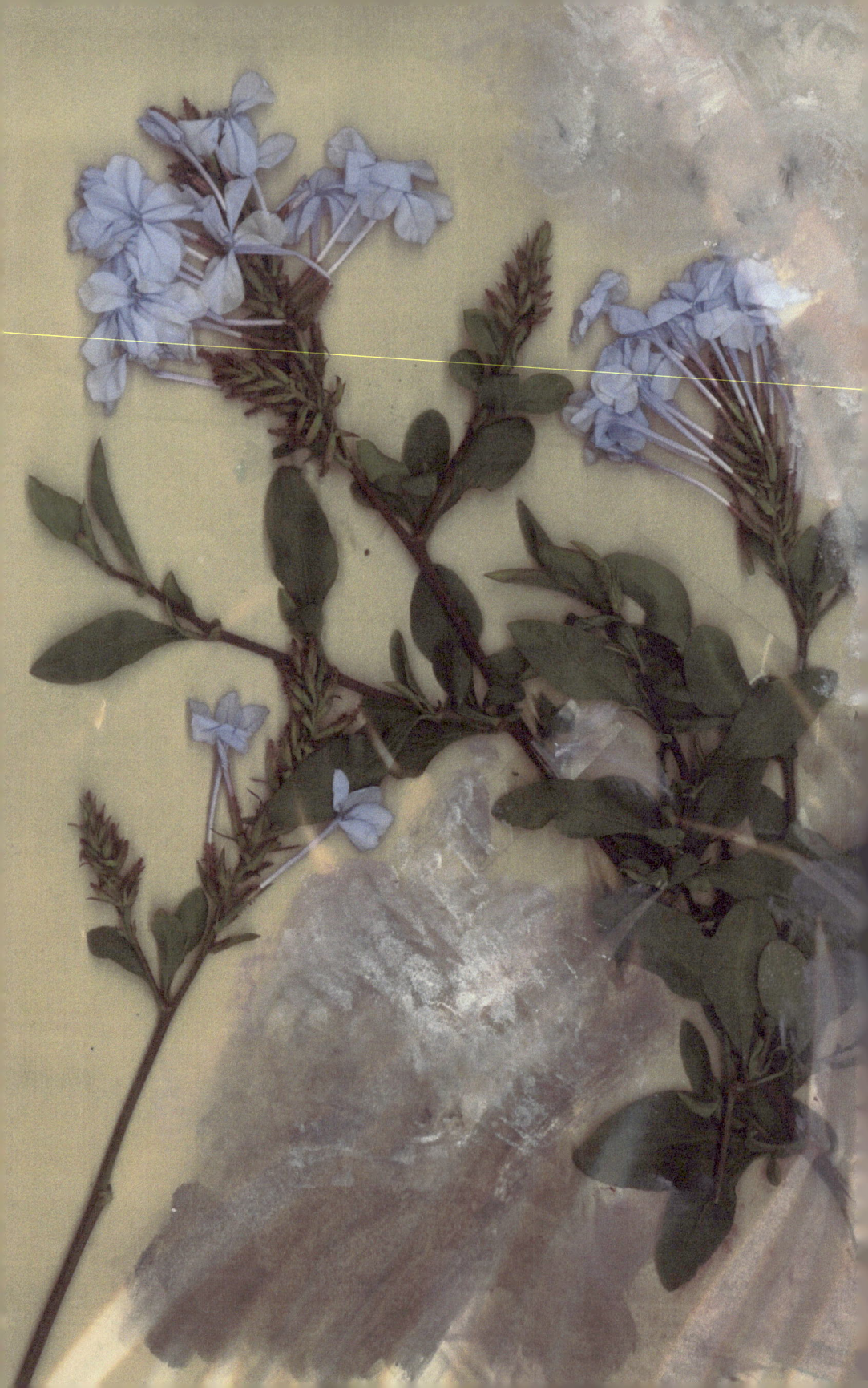

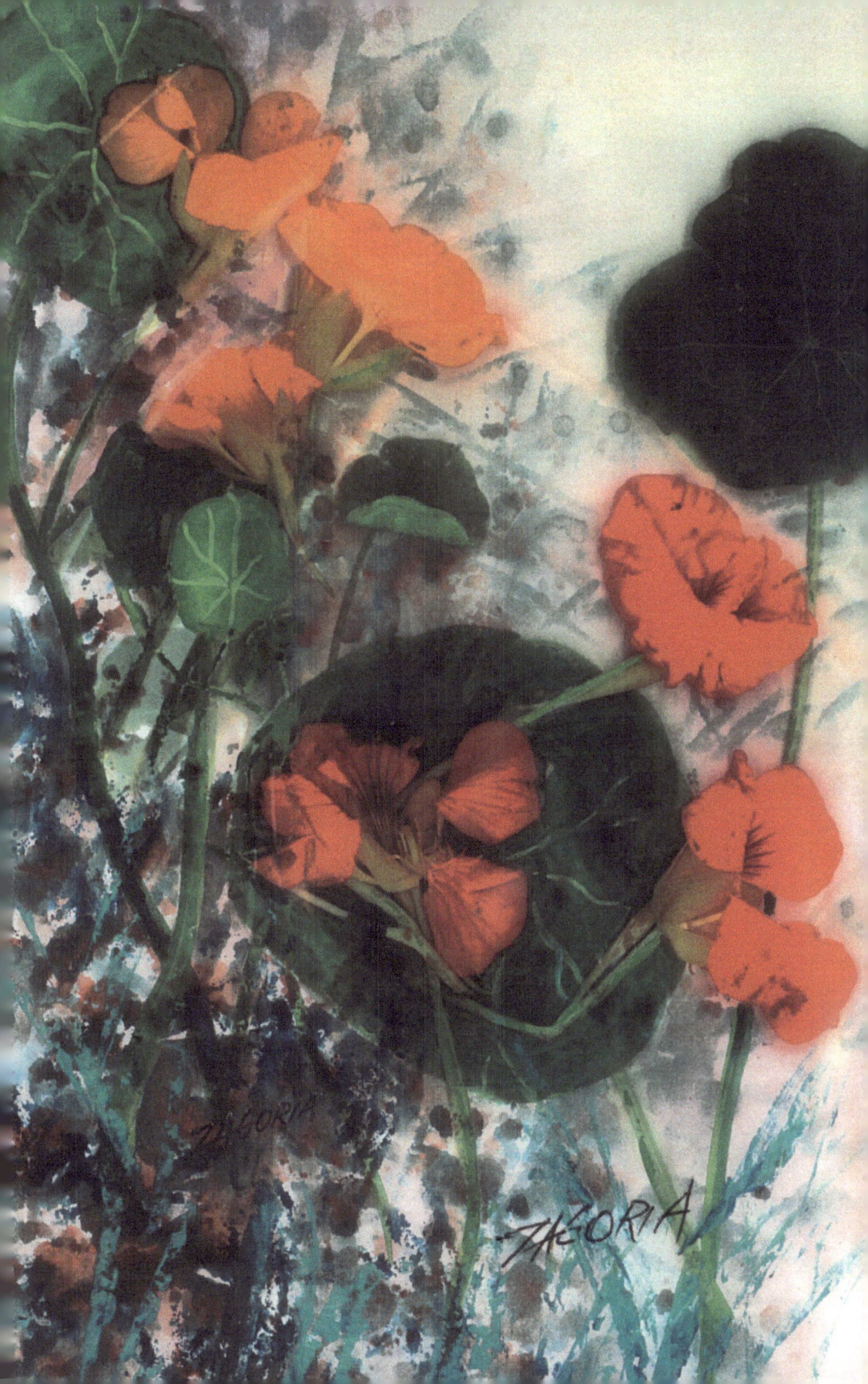

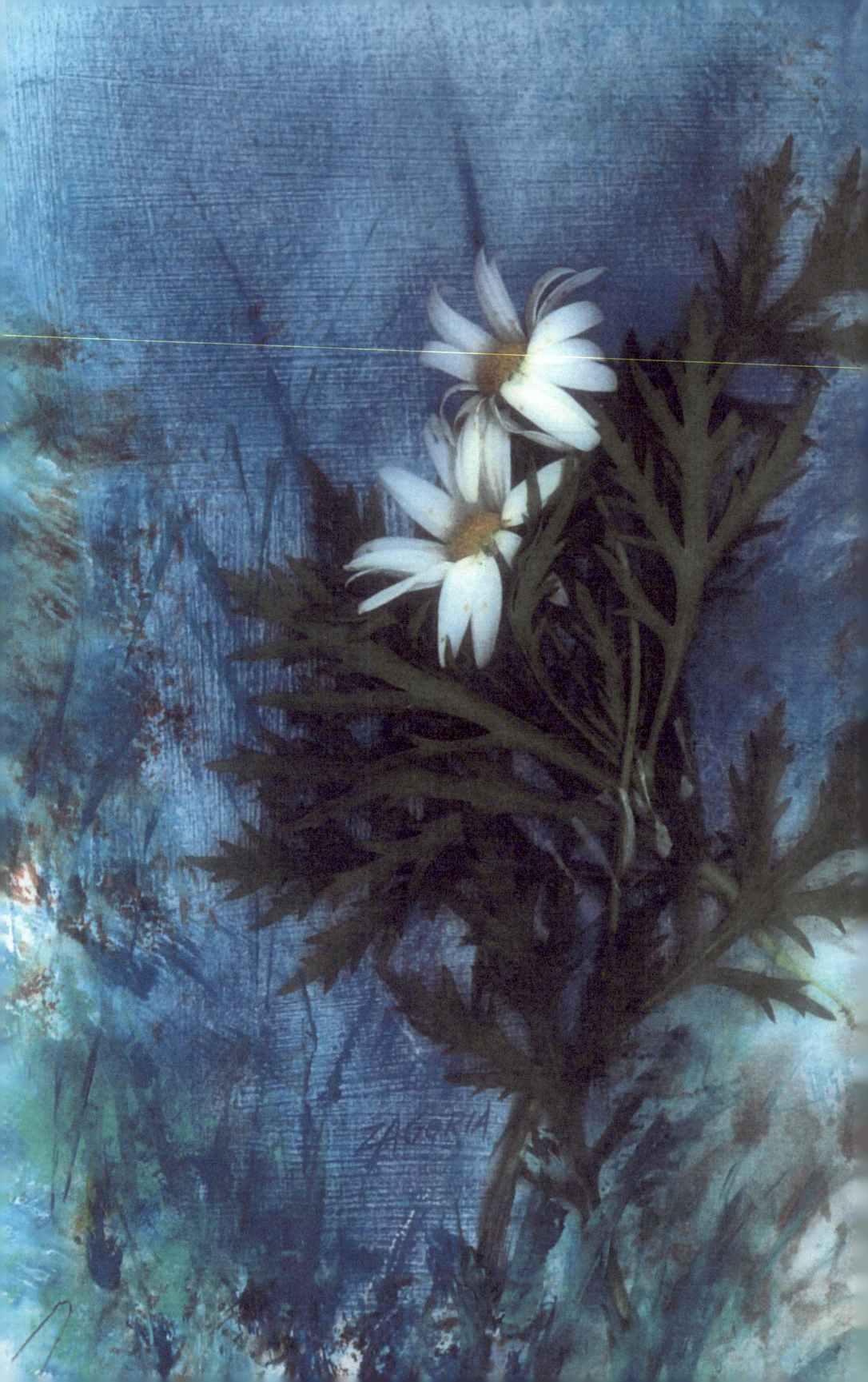

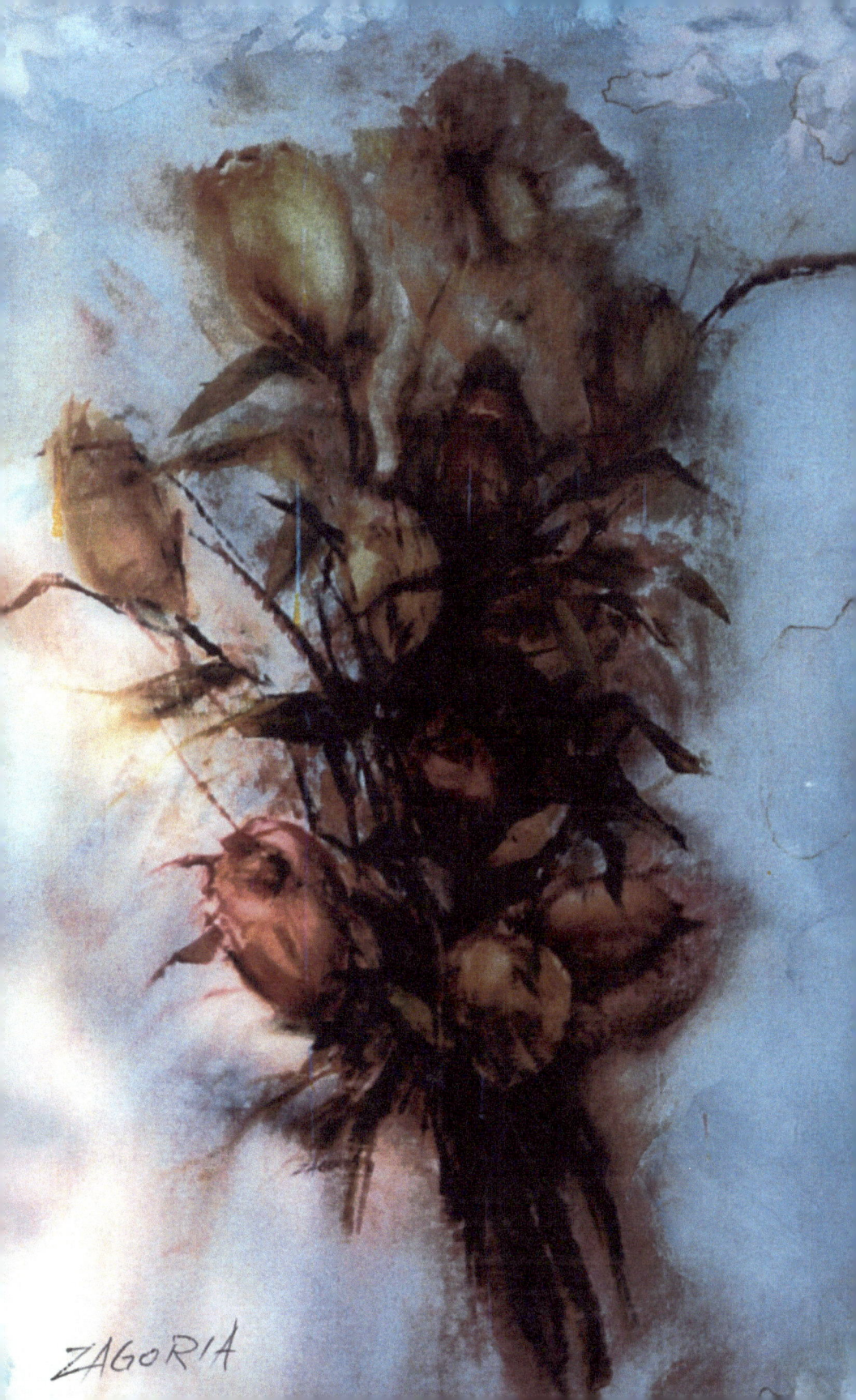

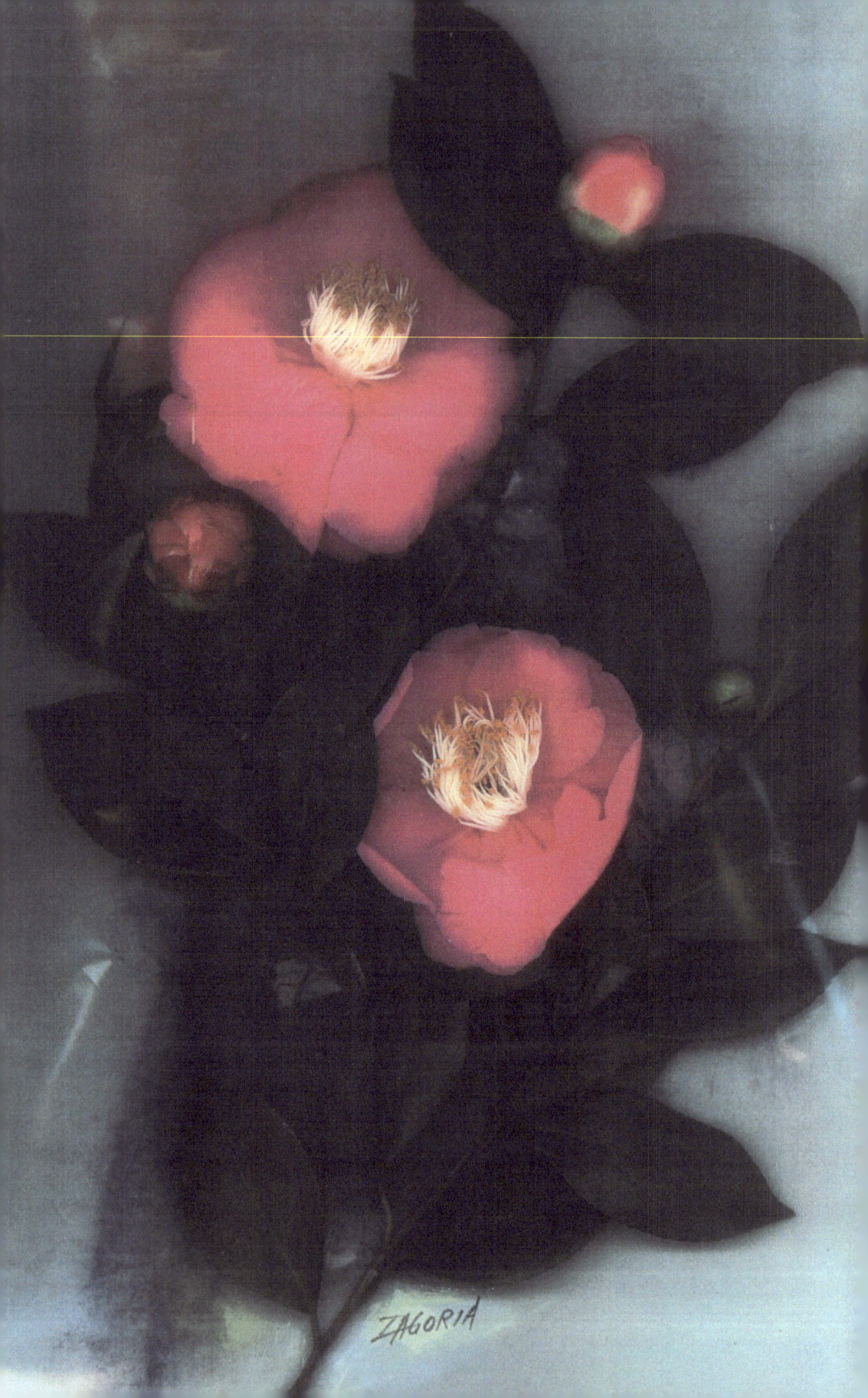

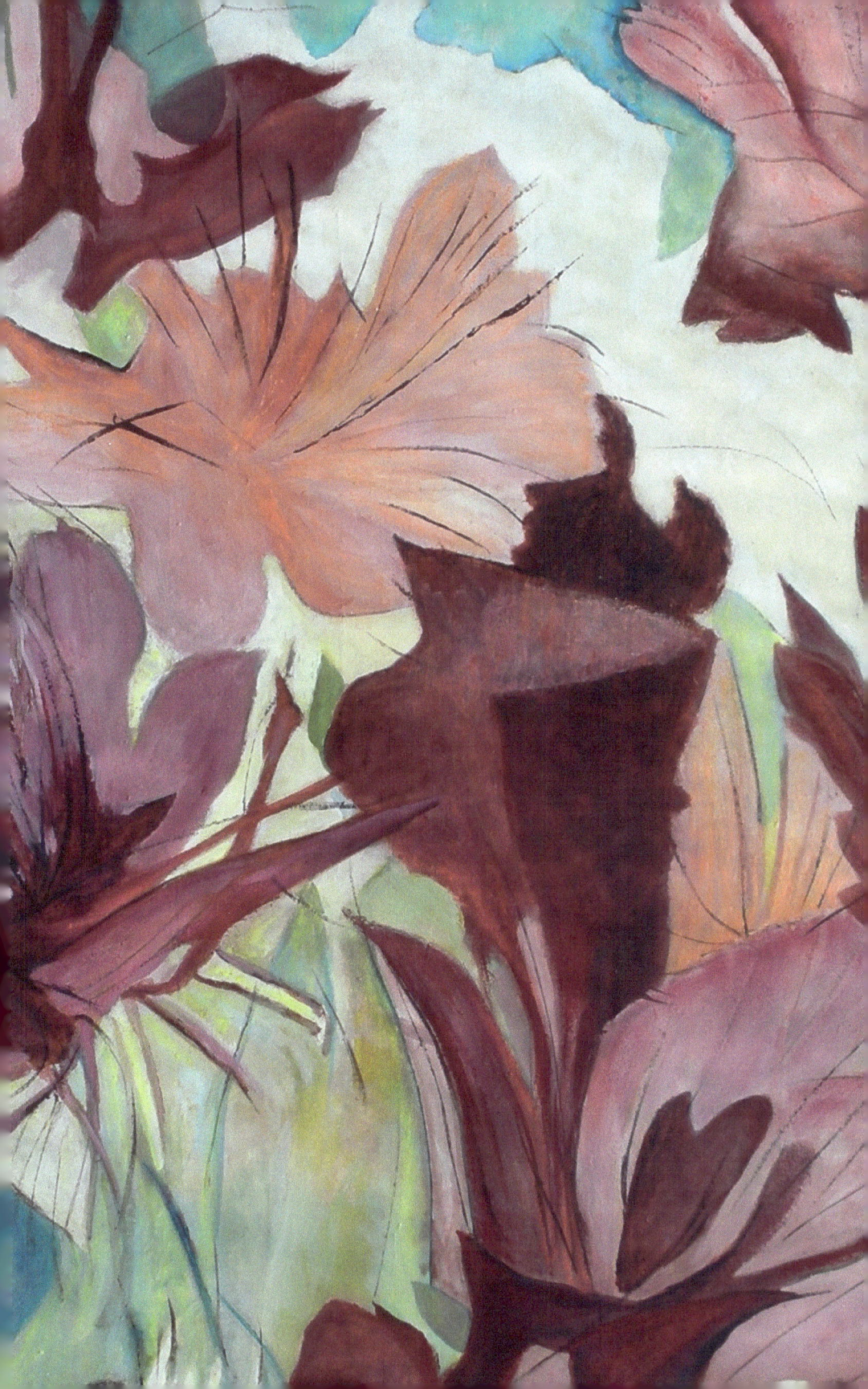

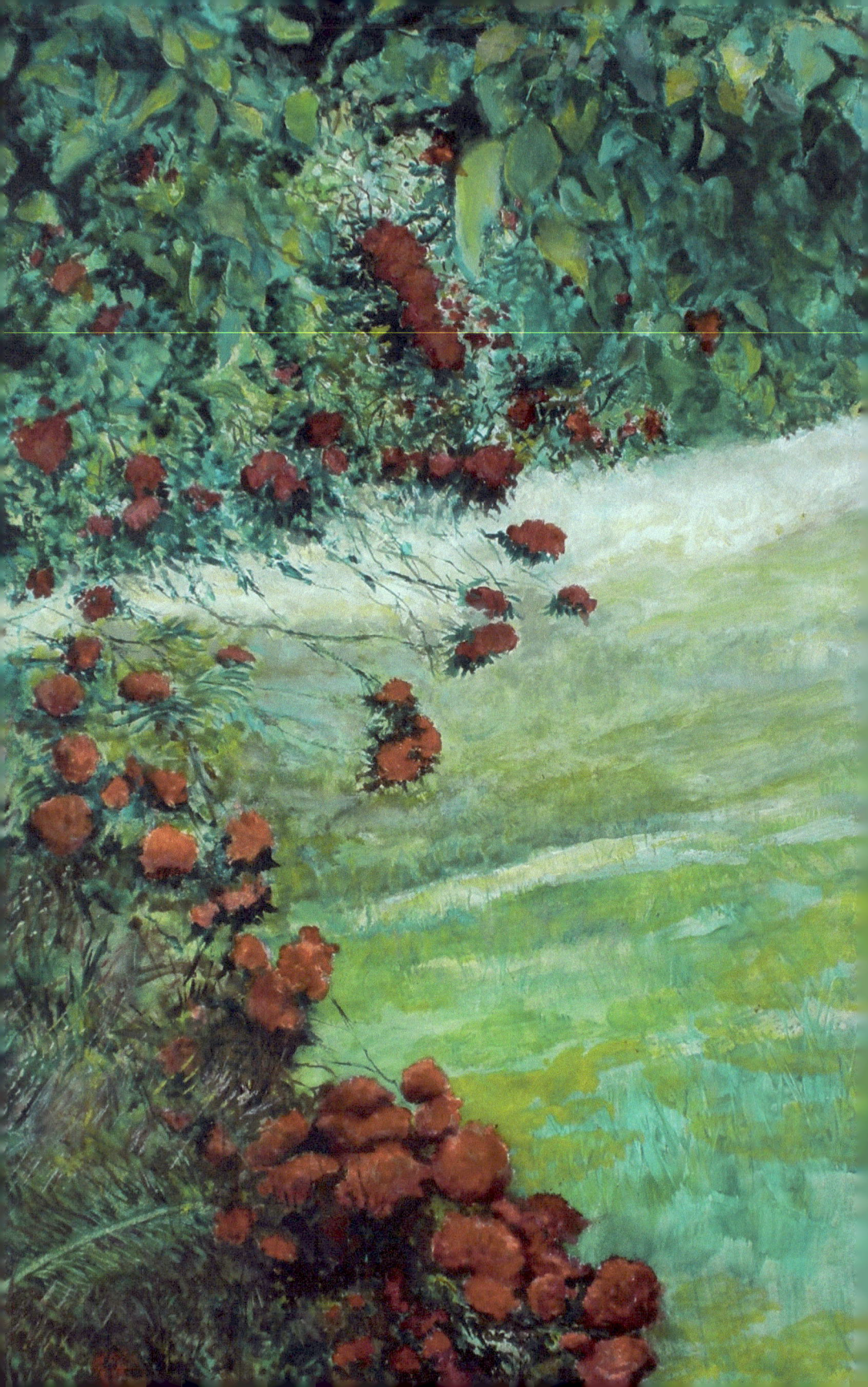

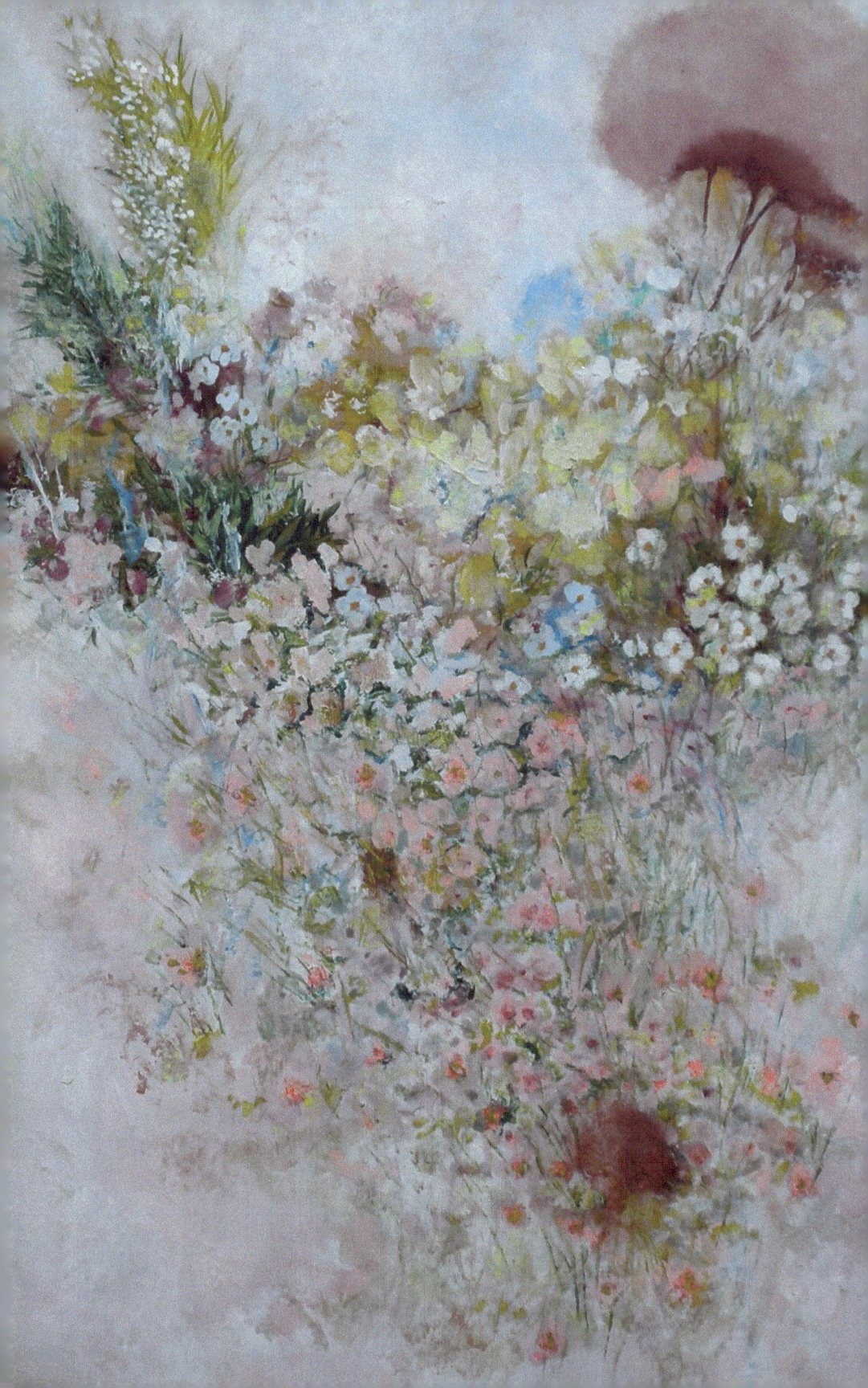

ELI ZAGORIA, THE ARTIST (1922-2013)

Eli was born in 1922 in Riga, Latvia and at age 14 emigrated to South Africa. While still at school he was encouraged with his art.

After leaving school he served in the South African Army in the Medical Corp and was captured in Tobruk, and was a prisoner of war in Italy and Germany. There, in Stalag IVB, he met another artist who was British, and a prisoner of war too. He was Eli's first art teacher and told Eli he should take art up as a profession.

After returning to South Africa in 1946 he was given a full three year scholarship in the Art College in Johannesburg and then volunteered to go to Israel and join the Israeli Army in the 1949 War of Independence. In the Israeli Army he once again was in the medical corp helping the wounded and sick.

Eli married Estelle Kaplan in 1949 and they spent seven years in Israel and over 23 years in Zimbabwe before returning to Johannesburg for 13 years. During this time in Johannesburg he did portrait sketches at East Gate shopping centre.

He came to Perth in 1992. He has two sons Michael and Ilan born in Israel and a daughter Karen born in Zimbabwe.

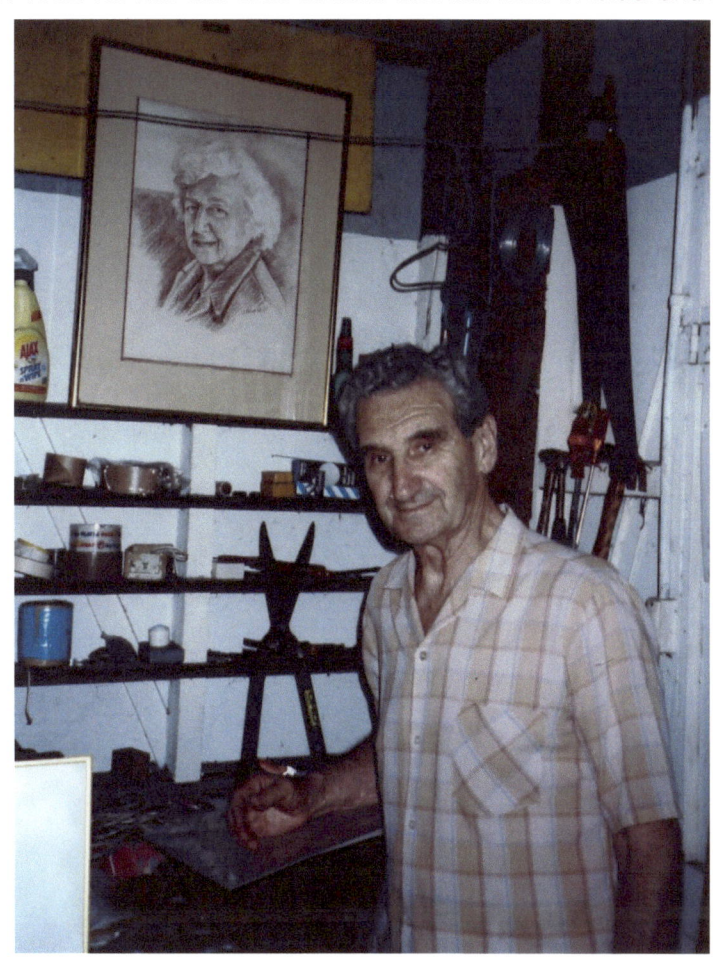

Eli, when he passed away early in 2013, still made his living from art, doing portraits and painting in his small studio at the back of his house. He estimated that he drew over 15,000 portraits over his lifetime.

Eli leaves behind his wife of 63 years, his three children and seven grandchildren.

Eli in his studio and workshop.

A portrait of his mother hangs on the wall

www.ingramcontent.com/pod-product-compliance
Lightning Source LLC
Chambersburg PA
CBHW041620180526
45159CB00002BC/946